A Child's View
of Christmas

Edited by
Richard & Helen Exley

Published by
The Pilgrim Press

Mark Peers, 7

Copyright © Exley Publications Limited 1980
First U.S. Edition, 1981.
ISBN 0-8298-0463-3
The Pilgrim Press
132 W. 31st St.
New York, N.Y. 10001.

Front cover drawing by Debra Toms
Back cover drawing by Lesley McIntosh, 9
Printed in Singapore by Dainippon Tien Wah Printing
(Pte) Ltd

2

Susan Coulthard, 14

*As long as there are children there will be
Christmas. They help us to go on believing in
the spirit, the sharing and the fun of Christmas.*

*I'd like to thank the children and their
teachers who helped us to create this book. For
me, they really captured the joy and the
innocence. All the work is absolutely genuine
and by children – even the spelling mistakes!
So, in every way this is their book. For you.*

Helen Exley

3

I wish you a presenty Christmas

Dinah Levy, 7

I wish you a Fathery Fathery Christmas

Terence Lee, 7

Julie Riegal, 7

My wish for you

I wish you joy
Love with your friends,
Happiness in your work,
Fortune with your salary,
Pleasure in your walks,
Well being in your dwelling,
Health in your body
Beauty in your self,
Delight in all,
Kindness from your friends,
Excellence in all you do,
Courage to do all well,
Determination to get things right,
And tender love from all.
Katie Mitchell, 14

Will Christmas never come?

I can't wait for christmas. I would just wish that
christmas would come quicley.   *Sarvjit Gill, 11*

I count the days, hours and even minutes.   *Susanne Elia*

When Christmas comes a tingley comes over all of me.
                                        Iain Whitaker, 12

Even the word Christmas makes me feel different
inside.   *Catherine Potter, 14*

What is Christmas?
It is my tummy rumbling tumbling
Round and round
Nearly falling
To the ground.   *Lisa Lewis, 8½*

Mommy, Mommy, look what I've found...   *Tracey Doran*

Christmas is looking under mom's bed and watching the piles of presents grow. *Christopher Jones, 10*

1..2..3...as the street lights light up the street and the house-lights shine through the cosy house windows, the smell of *Christmas* is near. The smell of baking cakes and pies and of roasting chicken for the big day is becoming greater and greater, the excitement of opening presents builds up. The Christmas carol records are on and the last rush for buying gifts is done. Time is nearly here, just a few more hours then everything can burst open for the day...
Wait, just wait. *Penny Smith*

I get some presents before Christmas and I pile them under the Christmas tree in the middle of the landing. When I pass the landing to wash my face I feel excited because I really think it's Christmas I shake them and I feel them I shake the ones that say Sophie. When it is Christmas I get excited. *Sophie, 6*

Christmas is the time of year when your observation should be at your best, especially when relatives and presents arrive. Eavesdropping devices are designed and you must remember where presents were hidden last year. In my case, this is easy. In our household nothing much can be kept secret to me anyway. *Philip Cowhig, 10*

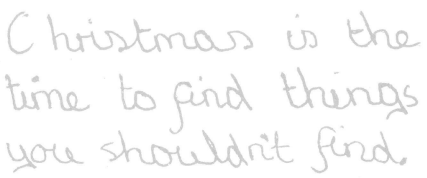

Christmas is the time to find things you shouldn't find.

Jeanette Freeman

Up go the decorations

About a week before Christmas my mom always buys
balloons. My dad has to blow them up because if my
mom blows them up she will faint. My dad does not like
blowing them up himself because it makes his ears go
red and we laugh.
Nattalie Page, 8

All the excitement and joy is upon us again.
Making the Christmas desserts and cookies.
The steam is rising, the pots are bubbling over in their
excitement.
The children think Christmas is never coming.
The parents cannot wait for it to be over.
Going to bed on Christmas Eve, so happy you cannot
get to sleep.
Philomena McNicholas, 13

The most thrilling thing is buying presents. After I have
got the presents I have to wrap them up and this is
where I can help my mother. Sometimes I help and
sometimes I hinder.
Karen Hirst, 10

The best thing is decorating the tree but I wish I was
taller because I have always wanted to put the angle on
the top.
Angela Miller, 10

Christmas is the time of year
when my Dad falls of
his step ladder trying to put
up the decoraltions.

Dariush Nejad, 8

8

Lorraine Kilby, 5

9

Elspeth Marshall, 9

Christmas, a time for
peace and goodwill,
and Christmas Shopping.

Andrew Twigg, 12

Peace and goodwill?

The agony of Christmas shopping, is it really worth it?
Children Screaming, and mothers occassionally
swearing. Pushing Jostling fighting and grabing. Bags
and Boxes flying every where. People pushing you with
carts and all they say is sorry and in the back ground
all can hear are the registers going ping.
Then up to the counter you go pushing and Jostling to
and fro. "76 dolars please" the assistent said.
Unwillingly you part with that horrible sum.

Paul Mason, 11

Not many people like Christmas shopping. One can get
serverely injured such as legs being cut by maniac
drivers and being stabbed in the back by
umbrellas. You weave towards the register like a
running back. You fight your way onto a bus or train.
Its no joke trying to swing like an ape from the
overhead handholds while clutching an armful of
packages. When finally reaching your destination, tired
and wounded, you are glad Christmas is only once a
year.

Paul Rogers, 12

Paul Mason, 11

Is he really real?

Last year I heard santa claus knocking on the door
Daddy let him in and I saw him in my bedroom with
his red coat on I kept my eyes shut.   *David Skidmore, 5*

I always try to stay awake to see who puts the presents
there. But I always fall asleep and never find out.
                                          Mark Levett, 9

Scott O'Brien, 7

I think Santa Claus is a kind old man taking toys to boys and girls all over the world I saw him down the town and he showed me skochtape on his beard.

Jayne Roberts, 5

One day at Xmas Eve we put out some sherry for Santa claws and wrote a letter and he replied in my Mommys handwriting.

Claire Senior, 7

Dear S. Clause Esq,

...Please don't bring another game of master mind. I have got four from last Christmas. And please could you bring me a bike instead of seven pairs of socks.

Howard Eggleston, 11

...Why didn't you send me the motor bike I asked for last year. With inflation, interest, Income tax and salary you now owe me two motorbikes a pair of front forks, a fuel tank, an engine and two wheels.

Richard Strike, 12

...I know, and I speak for all of the country, that we were looking forward to Christmas. But what's all this about the reindeers' strike, the North Pole Toy Manufactors' strike, the air strike, you can't fly, the truck strike, so your new sledge won't arrive on time. The cleaners' strike, so you can't get your reindeer skin coat back on time. I think this is disgraceful. What is the world coming to?

William Campbell,12

Dear Santa
Thank-you very much for last year's million but the country is in a bad way so I need another one

Yours Hoppfully
The President

John Bowron, 12

I bet you got a massure bill at the end of Chrismas

Richard Turner, 8

Miles Hutchinson, 12

15

Dear Santa Claus:

            Please may I
have a girls World and a Sindy
caravan and Will you come to our
Shool Party It is on the 19th
I look Forward to seeing you
Love Lucie. XXXXXXXX..

Lucie Cutts, 7

16

Dear Santa

...I am sorry that I have not written all year around but mommy says you are only in at Christmas.

Tracey O'Leary

...I some times wonder how you now what I want. Please will you fill my little fireplace Christmas stocking with candy? I am very shy of you but I hop you don't mind.
from Geoffrey
PS. Are you true?

Geoffrey Kyte, 8

...I hope you have time to rest after delivering all the presents. Love from Sally XXX

Sally Collins, 7

...Please will you come to our School party. The address is School 13 McLean Ave, Yonkers, New York,NY. Love from Victoria XXXXXXXXXXXXXXX

Victoria Wakefield, 7

...Please can I have just one teddy bear this christmas, nothing else but a teddy bear
from Sophia
PS. Please can teddy have a portable TV to keep teddy amused when I'm at school?

Sophia Jones

We will have a botl of wehe and some caks
Pleas well you not let my dad get them.
from Ian

Ian Thomas, 8

17

Saleem Jivraj, 9

Caught in the act

One Christmas Eve when I was eight or nine, I thought I'd try to catch Santa. So I got some black thread and tied one end round the handle on my dresser, and the other end to the string on a bell hanging on a nail on the wall. Later that night the door opened. I wasn't asleep but I pretended to be. Santa (or so I thought) walked slowly and quietly across the room, carrying a light. He didn't see the black thread. He tripped over the edge of the mat, through the thread attached to the bell and landed on something soft — me. I got a shock when I saw who it was. *Christine Hindmarsh*

I like watching out for you-know-who to break his neck falling down the chimney. We leave some beer and pies for Santa Claus. My father said to me last year "I, whoops, Santa Claus enjoyed them." *Lloyd Richards, 10*

I like christmas because he always comes, even when you don't believe in him

Susan Hyland, 14

19

Christmas Eve

I was so excited that night that I couldn't get to sleep.
All night I kept getting out of bed and brushing my
teeth just for an excuse. I don't know how many times I
brushed my teeth but I know my gums were sore.
Finally I got to sleep somehow. *Loraine Cook, 12*

A few years ago I was sent up to bed early with my
brother so we would not be like bears with sore heads in
the morning. *Tamsin Handy, 11*

On Christmas Eve you can pretend you are asleep and
get up and peep inside the parcels. My family wrap the
parcels up so tightly that you can't open them so you
give up trying and go back to bed. *Jean Ward, 9*

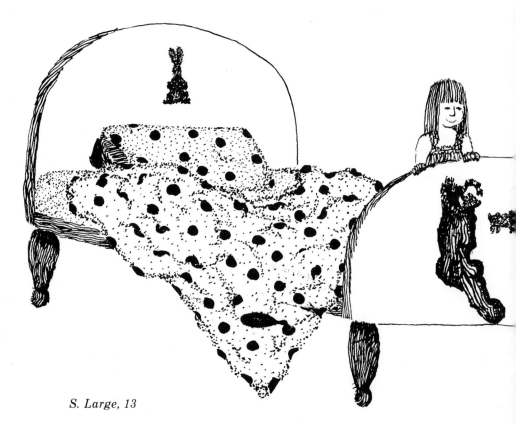

S. Large, 13

20

Then comes the exciting part. I drag my worn out mother up the stairs and into her bedroom where she gives my brother and I our stockings, and sends us running to our beds. Sleep trys to come but never does. At last at about 12 o'clock it comes and is welcome. The next thing I know is I am slowly slowly awaking. I automatically dig with my toes to see if Santa Claus came, yes! he had and it was very heavy too. I try to go back to sleep but it is impossible. So I quickly switch on the light, heave my stocking up and examin the presents, as best I can through the tissue, as it is a house rule not to open them before I go into my parents' room. I then try to get to sleep, every now and again digging with my toes to make sure my stocking is still there. Sleep never seems to come and I become thoroughly impatient and excited. At last 7.30 am comes and I leap out of bed, career down the passage and get my brother then. We both race along the corridor to my parents' room where we shout Christmas Greetings to one another and start tearing the tissue off our presents. This is the moment that I was waiting for all year round.

Louisa Bouskell, 11

The snow is falling,
The rain pouring,
The light dimming,
But crystals shimmering,
Everywhere in bleakness lays,
Except from houses, rays
Of hope, joy and love,
Filter through the darkness.
People singing,
Praises ringing,
Church bells chiming,
Street lights shining,
Streamers flying, high and low,
As through the night
The parties go.
Everyone is happy, full of love,
For the Christmas tide has arrived.

Teresa Cox, 14

it must be
horrible in
the
Chimney.
there must
be a lot of
Soot. I w
wonder why
he doest
come
through
the door

Brett Page, 6

Lucy Glasser, 7

A preoccupation with chimneys

Santa used to come through my mums chimney then she blocked it up so hes comming through the letter box.

Mark Aers, 7

David Gisby, 7

santa claus can Not come Down the chimney if he is fat. When santa claus come's down the chimney I wondor how he get's back UP again. Teresa Wipperman, 6

Hooray! It's Christmas morning!

When I get up, I deliberately sleep walk. I feel my stocking. Yahoo! I cry, it is Christmas Day!

Richard Sutton, 10

When I wake up I go to my brother, wake him up and say "Merry Christmas have you opened your stocking yet" all in one breath. He has usually opened it hours ago.

Sarah Sharpe, 13

When it was in the morning I saw toys and I got out of my bed to awake my brother. He is fat and lazy so I dragged him out of bed. Then he washed. It was only a little wash because we were too exsited.

Lee Francis, 10

Christmas is the only day when children get up early without being told too.

Simon Morgan, 10

On Christmas day I get up early at 5 o'clock. I wake my sister up then we go charging into my moms room. We have to jump on their bed to get *them* up.

Norman Robb, 9

In the morning, about 6.00 a.m. my will-power could stand the temptation no longer and I started to undo the presents but I woke Mom up because wrapping paper makes the most terrible crackling noise. I suppose it's made that way to stop children waking up the whole household.

Tracy Wadsworth, 12

On chrismtas day about 3.00. clock I Wake up and then Wake my mom It is chrismtas. I dont no why I do it.

Donna Smith, 10

Erley in the morning me and my brother sneek down stairs and going in to the ~~twing~~ liveing room and trieing to gess what present weve got in the dork. Then we give up and ask ~~as or~~ mun if we can open ~~or~~ presents ~~bey~~ thise time its about there o'clock

Alun Trower, 10

S. Cook, 9

The happiest day of the year

For a child, Christmas is a thrill.
Glass satin balls dangle at different lengths,
streams of sparkling tinsil are weaved
in and out, through the prickey tree.
Snow is wrapped around the tree like floating mist.
Fairy lights twinkle like colored sequins.
Presents are piled beneath the tree, all wrapped up in
glorious colored paper, just waiting to be opened.
Carols can be heard far and near.
Bursting balloons quiver on the walls.
The smell of Christmas dinner; roast potatoes, lean
turkey, brussel sprouts and cranberry sauce lingers in
the air throughout the day.
This is Christmas through children's eyes. *Sherrie Norris, 15*

Christmas is a time for happiness, pure happiness.
Roger Swaby, 10

If you don't like Christmas you've got to be nuts!
Howard Dodd, 10

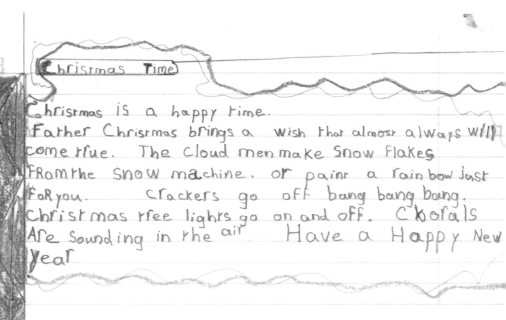

Christmas Time

Christmas is a happy time.
Father Christmas brings a wish that almost always will
come true. The Cloud men make Snow Flakes
From the Snow machine. Or paint a rainbow just
For you. Crackers go off bang bang bang.
Christmas tree lights go on and off. Chorals
Are sounding in the air. Have a Happy New
Year

Peter Smith, 8

Caroline Hurst, 5

Toys! Toys! Toys!

Although it sounds rather greedy, I think the bit I like most of all is when we all sit round the tree and open our presents.
Minette Hill, 11

First I open my small presents and then I open my medium size presents and then I open my biggest presents.
Emma Bridge, 9

We Sometimes get big big toys and cars. I can have big toys from my mom and dad. I can have a big big big big big big toy, aS big aS people.
Emma Warren, 7

When I open the presents, WHOOPEE! That makes me smile.
Pushpa Karat, 10

On Christmas day I am very happy. Because of the snow and Because I get presents. I get too many presents at Christmas. But I do not tell my mommy or my daddy.
Paul Chesterton, 7

I got a teddy one christmas and it was mine No body touched it just me. I hugged it and cuddled it I still got him now and he still Mine.

Sara Watson, 13

Jackie Healy

Happiness is lying in the bath writing a list of Christmas presents

Alison Connolly, 10

At home, because I am the youngest, I get the most presents although I am the naughtiest girl in the school I think. But I can be good.

Natalie Stewart-Clark, 8

The other exciting part is opening the presants and wondering what it is and Filling the present and shaking to see if it makes a noise and the thrill of seeing whats in side like a Annual all or record or camra somthing like that.

Susan Best, 10

Somehow you know that giving should be more fun than receiving but it isn't.

Charlotte Beattie, 10

HAPPINESS is FATHER christmas having difficulty taking off because hs helicopter is heavy with PreaSents

Simon Marcantoni

Giving is fun

I find great pleasure in rooting around at flea markets, and carefully ticking off names on my thousands of Christmas lists. I usually start thinking about Christmas presents in September, and begin buying and making things in November. This is the time my mom dreads! My bedroom is usually in chaos, with tell-tale pieces of glitter and wrapping-paper strewn all over the floor. She can't even tidy-up, because every cupboard, box, in fact everything everywhere is full of packages, big and small. But best of all, is when I give the presents. Normally, people don't expect me to have bothered, and it is lovely to see the surprise on their faces.

Susan Howe, 10

It's easy to give a present, but it's not easy to give what they nied the most that is love and time and affection but if you are too late do not be to worried because there is another Christmas.

Jonathan Hempstead, 8

I like opening the presents all my mom likes is seeing our faces when we open them.

Claire Schauerien, 9

The most presious gifts are love and life which money can not buy.

Philip Nye, 10

I like everyone saying "Thats just what I wonted and all the "oo os" and "ahhhs" and "You shoudn't haves"

Diane Upcraft, 11

Suzanne King, 7 ▶

A family time

Christmas is made up of the little things that really
matter like stockings and leaving Santa Claus a
glass of milk and a cookie. Giving our parents
breakfast in bed at six o'clock in the morning. Going to
midnight mass and seeing all the little children falling
fast asleep after the first five minutes of the service.
Then coming home in the snow (if we're lucky) to a cup
of coffee and a cookie in front of the log fire.
The Christmas dinner — roast turkey, ham, potatoes
and all the trimmings, hot burning Christmas pudding
scorched holly on the top. Brandy and rum butter —
and Mom has been a little too liberal with the booze!
Then, there are always cookies and coffee which you
just have to find room for. Then presents, the highlight
of the day in the children's eyes. Giving and receiving
are just as fun as the Christmas tree slowly loses its
presents to eagerly waiting hands.
After that a long pause when the grown-ups have a
sleep and wonder how they could have eaten so much —
then Mom appears with tea and the Chistmas cake
which you have to squeeze in somewhere because Mom
will be offended if you don't.
Then a long walk for everyone and then carol singing
in the evening to help the children go to sleep after a
lovely Christmas day. *Morag Forse, 14*

To be happy is the secret of life. To wake up on
Christmas morning and know that you are loved makes
you very happy. *Penny Knight Hamilton, 12*

Dear mommy
Thank-you very much four the kind presents that you
give me and I like them very much. and I lik my guinea
pig and it makes me go to sleep. and I like you very
much and I hope you love me as well. and you are very
kind to me when I am poorly and you make me happy.
You are very lovely indeed and I am looking forward to
christmas.
Love Sally *Sally Anderson, 6*

When it is Christmas I can see the smile in my mom and dad's faces and it makes me happy to see them smile. Perhaps this is the biggest gift in life.

Tracey Hillman, 8

Kate Epton, 8

Christmas is kissing
relatives you
don't like.

Pamela O'Brien, 15

Steven Nunn, 13

Catastrophies

I wish you joy when battling through the milling
crowds with an armful of heavy bags when Christmas
shopping.
I wish you joy when the sticky tape lives up to its name
and sticks to everything . . . except the wrapping paper.
I wish you joy when you buy a cassette tape for your
friend and find out that she hasn't got a cassette
recorder.
I wish you joy when the enormous Christmas pie
burns to a cinder on the great day.
I wish you joy when you have just put the finishing
touches to the Christmas tree and the cat knocks it over.
I wish you joy when at the end of a long Christmas
day, you sink into a nice warm bed and realise the cat
is howling at the back door. . .   *Sarah Guest, 12*

Christmas
is when
the
dog is
sick

Charlotte Fall, 14   *Sarah Wood*

35

There was a young lady
named White.
Who sang carols with all
of her might

She would ring someones bell
And warble Noel
Till they begged her
for silent night

Daxesh Mehta, 11

Fiona MacVicar, 10

Sometimes I can not decide what to buy them so to settle the matter, I buy them something they need, not nessecserilly wants, but is going to get it. *Jeremy Slater, 12*

I like seeing the Christmas dessert blow up when Mom lights the brandy. We all run about like lunatics.
Richard Sutton, 10

We all look forward to Christmas time as a time of giving and helping, of kindlyness and of celebrations, of good will, but when the time comes we all crowd round the television. *John Bowron, 12*

Christmas is waiting for all the grown-ups to finish lunch so that all the children can get on with the presents. *Carey Nason, 13*

Christmas time is a very happy time. Even Adults are happy at Christmas *Stephen Shears, 12*

Christmas is mums saying don't fight this is the season of good will.

Linda Dickinson, 10

Lucy Ellis, 9

My Christmas	Mom's Christmas
decorations	climbing up on a wobbly ladder, probably falling.
a Christmas tree	pine needles and tinsel all over the carpet.
lots of food	preparations and loads of dishes to be washed.
crackers	crumpled paper everywhere.
presents	money down the drain.
sweets	indigestion and tooth-ache.
parties	late nights, and driving back through the dark.
snow to play in	getting soaked and frozen whenever outside.

Sarah Forsyth

Lois Pass

Christmas is a happy time, not so much for grown-ups

Angela Harrington, 10

Janine Loehr, 12

We better be good, this is God's House.

Jennie Di Gaetano, 12

Let's go in and see Santa.

Sonnin Dahl, 8

Will Santa fit in that chimney?

Thrin Stuart, 7

Age 11 Angela
Georgiou

Christmas is the season
when the stomach
works overtime.

Susan Hyland, 14

Eat, drink and be sick

Unhappiness is weight-watching at Christmas.

Elisabeth Lumb, 13

Turkey for you, Turkey for me,
Turkey for lunch, Turkey for supper
Turkey for you, Turkey for me.

Samantha Kelly, 10

The Christmas dinner's on the table,
Eat some more if you are able;
Plenty there so help yore-self,
Alka-seltzer on the shelf.

Philip Luck, 12

I dont like christmas frutcak because it make my fore
head go all hot and stuffy and I have a shiver down my
back The spices go up my nose an make me sneeze and
it lookes steeming hot and curranty.

Ruth Apery, 7½

I fed my Christmas
Pudding to my Cat because
I do not like it and
I only wanted the money
My Poor Cat was Sick.

Emma Goble, 8

43

Too commercialised?

Maybe poorer people know the true meaning of Christmas. Christmas today is more of a sales campaign than anything else. Maybe people will learn to enjoy Christmas as it should be when they become older or at some time in their life when they are a bit short of cash.

Michael Carroll, 14

I have been dying to say that Christmas is too comercialised

Susan Payn, 15

Caroline Findlow, 12

Money v Jesus

Bright lights shining,
The laser beaming,
Drawing people like the star of Jesus.
People talking, shop lights calling,
"Buy Christmas here!
Here! Here! and there!
Christmas for sale!"
The ads on TV
"Buy this for Ellie."
It all is fantastic,
Magnificent, elastic.
But where has Christ gone?
Has Mary left too?
Christmas is business,
Jesus has left us.

Rachel Hopkins, 13

CHRISTMAS is a time for HAPPINESS It doesn't matter if you get an apple or a pony for your present!

It's still Christ's Birthday

Ursula Scrimegour, 9

More than just presents

If I asked you just suppose,
What Christmas means to you,
Would you say it's good for business,
Mom puts on a good spread too,
Or would you say it means the peace
   that Jesus brings to me.

If I gave you a Christmas wish,
I wonder what it would be,
A cuddly elephant, a big posh car, a truck
   or a chimpanzee,
Or would you ask for the atmosphere,
Of Christmas time all around the year.   *Jill Warburton, 12*

Christmas, to me, seems to have lost all meaning. It is
really a time to celebrate the birth of Jesus Christ. But
now, it seems only a time for presents (that you don't
really need), turkey, Christmas parties and drinking
(and getting drunk); and people groan at the thought of
Christmas because of all the presents they have to buy.
   Larraine Boyce, 15

Christ was born in a small drafty stable. We now
spend Christmas in luxury, look at the gay decorations
and presents. We must try to remember the poverty
Jesus was born into.   *Jane Samples, 12*

Christmas is the time of joys
Not the pile of lovely toys
Nor the stocking full of goods
But when we do the things we should

Christmas is the time when she
Lay the baby on her knee
Rocked him gently to and fro
   because, like us, she loved him so   *Helen Merckx, 10*

I like christmas becouse You think about things.
   Donna Smith, 10

Karen Jones, 5

remember that tiny baby
who was like a refugee
– he had a stable with
no central heating

Stephen Petzke, 7

I Like chrismas because It is Jesus's birthday. he has the birthday we get the presents.

Joanne Hayes, 6

Mary and Joseph invented Carol singing. By going round asking is there any room to let.

Jamie Rowe, 10

CHRIST came to earh
to teach us to believe in God
And not to be naughty.

Nicola Channon, 9

49

Susie Hooper, 12

Happy birthday, Jesus

Frost-spangled twigs and sparkling stars
Shine like candles in the clear night.
Church bells ring, rippling through the darkness,
Still, somewhere in the mind a little grey donkey
    travels on.

Green holly is heavy with scarlet berries,
The innocent robin sleeps in its nest.
Hearts are holy with warmth and wine,
Still, somewhere in the soul a child is born.

Joanna Taylor, 14

On cristmas we feel happy and joyfull and very gretfull
for all the things we have got OK. Pepole and anties
and moms and dads and uncils and we feel like we are
being wathed biey Jesus and you feel like you are his
frend and befour you open your presints you say Happy
Birth Day Jesus.   *Mark Mould, 7*

Really it is one big birthday party for Jesus but as he is
not here to give him presents we give them to the people
we love instead.   *Mark Harvey, 8*

I wish you
A christ like
christmas

Claire Ellicott, 8   *Avril Tobin, 9*

It can be a sad time for some

Every year my mom usually told me a Christmas story from the Bible. Every year it was just as if I had heard the story for the first time and it was never old or something like "I have heard that before".
However this year it was a very sad year because one year ago my grandfather died and my mother was naturally very quiet. We were busy putting presents around the Christmas tree, when we suddenly found our mom was upstairs, so my sister and I went up and found our mom crying. I immediately thought of the message Christ tried to teach us — always be mild and humble and think, and Christmas should be a time of giving and not of receiving.
My sister and I put our arms around our mother, and tried in our small way to comfort her by telling her that our Christmas gift to her was our love. She smiled and said it was the loveliest Christmas gift she had ever received.
Richard Coelho

I was made an orphan in February. I can't get used to the fact that my parents are dead, I'll never see them again. Although the Matron sends us all a present from Mom and Dad it's not the same, you know it's not really from them. We all get a visit from the butcher, dressed up as Santa but even though his beard falls off like Daddie's used to do, it's not the same.
I hope soon I' ll be adopted, then presents really *will* be "from Mom and Dad" and not Matron. If I'm adopted then Christmas will be all normal, like everybody else.
Trina Rust, 11

My Iader of chrismtas this year is that all my famely stay at home and then CeleBrate. We did not last year. We didnt my mom went out drinking. *Christine, 11*

The only thing that I do'nt like about Christmas is getting new presents because I can only play with my dad and he is usely talking. *John, 7*

Lesley Hancock, 12½

christmas is the
loneliest day of the
year for a lonely
peson.

Tanya Fabbri, 14

53

S. Hudson

I am the poor

Christmas is a very nice time, but what about the poor, oh God give the poor food to eat and water to drink and houses to live in, like we have.   *Hassan Iftikhar, 9*

When I wake up on Christmas morning I usually just lie in bed and think about all those poor children who have no mother or father. They probably won't even have a Christmas turkey or any presents. Then there's all those poor men who are made to go to war, to fight for their country, they won't get a Christmas either.
After that I lie in bed and think about what I will get for Christmas maybe I will get some clothes, or plenty of sweets, or chocolates in boxes or maybe lots of games like Cluedo, Monopoly, battleships and lots of other games. But then while I'm lying in bed it all keeps coming back about those poor people who won't have Christmas.   *Arun Stobbart, 11*

Some children don't beleave in Jeasus but still Celerbrate Chistmas and still get presents. There are also poor people who do believe in Jesus and they don't get presents. i think that I am quiet lucky because I believe in Jesus, I celerbrate Christmas *and* I get presents.   *Nancy Sisson*

No christmas dinner have I
I am the poor
No presents have I
I am the poor
I am not like the upper crust
Christmas cheer
brandy to warm
turkey
roast pork
Crackling fire not me
I am the poor.

Danny King, 10

Old and alone

The old lady sits in her chair.
Listening to the ticking of the clock by the stair.
She thinks of Christmases past
And waking to find the Great Day come at last.

She'd loved those Christmases when she was young.
Sitting by the fire where her stocking was hung.
Opening presents her eyes shining bright.
The Christmas tree standing in glittering light.

But that was long ago, no one comes any more.
Not even to say "Happy Christmas" and knock on the door.
And so the old lady just sits in her chair.
Listening to the ticking of the clock by the stair.

Mariota Kiltermaster, 12

Christmas is for everyone, but old people
Are alone.
They need a helping hand, they need
A friend, they also need concern.
We never help, we just help ourselves.
When will we ever learn?

Penny Hogan, 13

Christmas in the life of an old woman

I see their happy little faces
As they bundle down the street.
Their scarves and little woolly hats.
I see them singing carols
With lanterns that light up the night
Their little mouths opening for every word,
And their eyes twinkling bright.
I watch them go home over the hills
Their lanterns fading dim
I look at myself by the fire
And wish I were as happy as them.

Shirin Syed, 12

Karen Johnson, 9

I want it to Snow On Christmas Eve
and on christmas day and boxing day
and every day. I want it six feet deep.
I want a blizzerd and
a snow storm and
frost underneath
as well.

Jason Webb, 8

Every November God collects all the white goodness from Heaven and throws it down on the world. If you wonder why snow does not snow so much as it used to it is because their is not enough goodness.

Gail Wilson, 11

Gina Oliver, 10

Imagine: life without Christmas

Life without Christmas would be a real drag. You wouldn't be able to stay awake on Christmas Eve and eat candys from your stocking until you feel sick.

Graham Munday, 11

Life without Christmas would be very booring indeed . . . but on the other hand you would not have to save up your pocket money to buy other people presents.

Philip Penn, 8

Caroline Speke, 13

Stephen Gibson, 9

The whole of every year would be dull if there Wasn't any Christmas day. I would miss eating Turkey, roast poatatoes, peas, gravy, Christmas pudding and custard. I would miss blowing up the balloons and scaring the life out of my mom by bursting them. *Justin Hammond, 8*

. . . there would be no such thing as Christianity because if Christ wasn't born all religion would have stayed pagan. *Graham Munday, 11*

If there wasnt any Christmas I would call it Nomas. People in Noland hang up their nomas stockings and go to bed. In the morning they would wake up and you should see their sad faces as they open their nomas presents and eat their nomas dinner. *Helen Robinson, 8*

If you never had Christmas you would have to play with the same toys over and again. *Kim Tagg, 8*

If we did'nt have a christmas we would have to call it nothing-mas day.
Mark Finch, 9

Mark Saunders, 9

John Adamson, 13

A Christmas message to someone I love

Dear Father Christmas,

When I was little there was always you to trust and rely on.
Every year you would come with your presents; books, sweets and toys.
But where are you now?
Gone, lost forever from my life.
Why? For the simple reason I am too old to be allowed to believe in you.
So, dear Santa, if you are real, grant that I never will be too grown-up to forget the real meaning of Christmas.

Love,

PENNY BROWN
St Gregorys High
School. 2.H.
AGE 13

Penny Brown. × × ×

63